I've got a hot-rod Ford and a two-dollar bill

And I know a spot right over the hill

There's soda pop and the dancin's free

So if you wanna have fun, come along with me.

From 'Hey Good Lookin', Hank Williams, 1951

ANDREW SHAYLOR
FOREWORD BY JERRY CHATABOX

Rockin'
The Rockabilly Scene

MERRELL
LONDON · NEW YORK

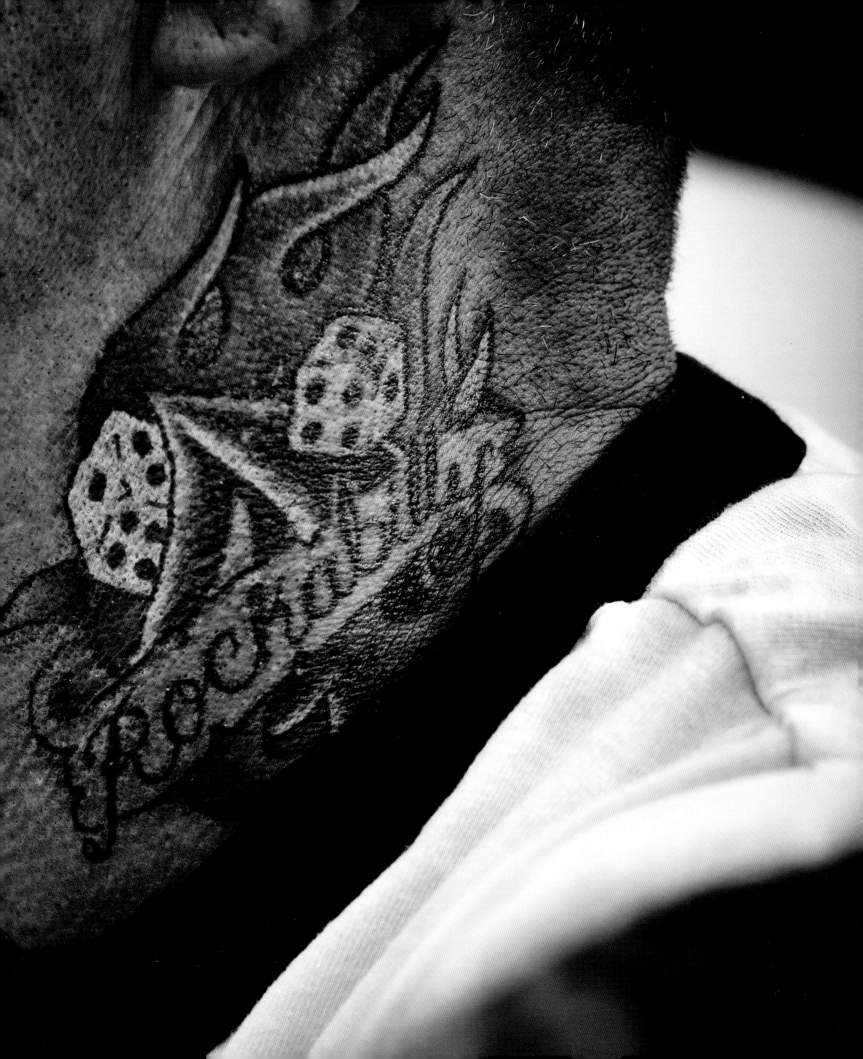

9 **FOREWORD** BY JERRY CHATABOX

16 **THE ROOTS OF ROCKABILLY**

28 **THE ROCKIN' SCENE**

36 *Rockin'*

192 **ROCKIN' EVENTS**

It's a sad fact that society generally celebrates the rich and famous, not the poor and obscure. We'll often know the names of the generals, but not those of the foot soldiers, and we usually learn the winning side's version of history, seldom the loser's. You could be forgiven for thinking that the only memorable popular-culture symbols to have come out of the 1950s were Marilyn Monroe, Elvis Presley and pink Cadillacs: these iconic images are repeated ad nauseam for the general public. But what else was there in that era, and what came before that? What and who were the influences behind those iconic images? What about the hundreds of singers and musicians who recorded at the same time as, or before, Elvis? The bands who played for the love of the music, not the money, the pioneers who started style trends, not followed them, the people who shaped an era in music and style but are now long forgotten by the media?

In a nutshell, the 'what came before' has become the cornerstone of the Rockin' scene, a scene that looks further and delves deeper into the rockabilly music produced in the main by small independent recording studios in the United States between 1950 and 1955. The Rockin' scene celebrates unsung heroes, and hero-worships singers and musicians who helped others to become rich and famous but were never themselves rewarded, financially or otherwise. Those true innovators made it possible for others to follow so much more easily in their footsteps.

People today often make the mistake of thinking that the era of their youth was the first to produce teenage rebellion – sex, drugs and rock 'n' roll. The 1960s, 1970s and 1980s are often cited as being ground-breaking eras; people still talk about the drug-fuelled 1960s or the punk-rock scene in the late 1970s as if they were unique. What they fail to realize is that all the taboos had already been broken long before.

In the 1970s, having hair dyed bright red was seen as being new and wild, yet Sonny Burgess was shocking audiences with his bright-red hair and wild stage show in the mid-1950s. The leather-clad Suzi Quatro of the 1970s owes a debt to Charline Arthur, who back in 1953 slid across the stage in cowboy-style trousers and belted out risqué songs about sleeping with her boyfriend. This was unheard-of for a female performer at the time, and outrage at her masculine clothes and raunchy material led to harsh criticism and to her being banned from auditoriums. But arguably the most obvious example to make the point is the world's first real rock star, Hank Williams.

Williams beats them all. A hard-drinking, drug-abusing, brilliant singer–songwriter whose songs are still played and copied to this day, he died of a drug overdose, in the back of a Cadillac outside a nightclub, while on tour in 1953 (his cause of death was officially recorded as heart failure). You want a rock star? He was the original. Plenty of other musicians with troubled souls have died tragically along the way, but I somehow doubt their music will still be played half a century after their death. And if it is, I doubt it will still sound as edgy, raw and exciting as the day it was made.

So it wasn't Elvis who started it all. He was there, of course, recording at the then virtually unknown Sun Studio in Memphis, Tennessee (the studio was almost the home of rockabilly, with Carl Perkins, Jerry Lee Lewis, Roy Orbison and Johnny Cash all having started their careers there, along with Jack Earls, Sonny Burgess, Ray Harris, Billy Lee Riley, Jimmy Wages, Warren Smith, Johnny Carroll … the list is seemingly endless). Elvis's early Sun singles are fine rockabilly, but they are not the songs he is known for today. Famously, his contract with Sam Phillips, who founded Sun Studio and Sun Records, was bought for a modest fee by RCA, and the company managed to take his raw energy and talent and package it, and sell it, much as is done with the packaged pop idols of today. Elvis had a huge hit in 1956 with 'Blue Suede Shoes', a song that was written

and originally recorded by Carl Perkins, a country boy like Elvis, but a few years older than him, more awkward and not as handsome or photogenic. Perkins was always going to be in Elvis's shadow, but he was the one who broke the mould, writing his own songs and playing simple searing guitar that was adored and later copied by the likes of the Beatles and the Rolling Stones. The 'Sun Sound' of Carl Perkins is regarded as classic rockabilly by many aficionados, and his archive of recordings is held in almost reverential awe by the scene. Yet in stark contrast to reactions to Elvis's death in 1977, when Perkins died (in 1998) the outside world took little or no notice.

1970s Revival

Twenty years after the original 1950s recordings of rock 'n' roll and rockabilly were made in the United States, Britain underwent a strange nostalgic rock 'n' roll revival. It was in the main led by the original 1950s Teds (Teddy Boys) and Rockers (bikers) and their children. I was fourteen at the time and had just heard Elvis and Buddy Holly on mainstream radio. I was completely hooked. The music and singing sounded so raw and powerful and urgent, nothing like the ridiculous manufactured glam rock in the charts.

We youngsters quickly discovered where this exciting music could be heard. We found clubs that would let us in (and sell us beer); if we got turned away because we were too young, we'd go and listen to the music from outside the toilet windows. We'd walk miles through the night if we missed the last bus or train, but it always seemed worth it. If we did manage to get into a club, there were girls, there were drinks, there were tough old tattooed Teds (best avoided) and always there were fights. It was a very volatile scene, with us young punchy kids entering the arena, keen to make a name for ourselves and thinking we knew it all, and the older crowd and the bikers and the long-haired rock 'n' roll fans in their flares, and the musicians with long hair and V-shaped rock guitars playing Chuck Berry songs deafeningly loudly. It all seemed crazily exciting. But it was also puzzling for us youngsters. For instance, some of the old Teds were very racist, yet they liked music by Chuck Berry, Little Richard, Big Joe Turner and all the fantastic (and mainly black) American doo-wop groups.

There was nothing authentic about this scene. Many of the Teds wore brightly coloured drape coats, which were a 1970s invention and had never been worn in the 1950s. The fashion was for hairsprayed quiffs, not hair grease. The musicians often had long hair, played modern instruments – sometimes even electric bass guitars – and performed a very 'heavy' form of rock 'n' roll. The alternative was the glam-rock version, which was simply a pathetic, cartoony interpretation of the real thing.

On reflection, it seems fairly clear that what made the biggest impact on the development of the Rockin' scene we recognize today, were the records the DJs played. In the mid-1970s, when I was first on the scene, anything was played: British rock 'n' roll from Cliff Richard and Tommy Steele, or classic tracks from Bill Haley, Little Richard and Elvis. But there were also bootleg singles being brought into the clubs by dealers who had bought originals from the United States, and we had the chance to hear Johnny Burnette, Charlie Feathers, Warren Smith, Lew Williams and the Collins Kids. These 1950s 'country rock', or rockabilly, tracks sounded very different from the mass-produced hits of their era, and we could not get enough of them. It was a stripped-down sound, just the bare essentials, often just a singer, a bass and a guitar. Drums were not always necessary, the upright bass (or bull fiddle) being slapped to produce the note and an added click, which was often the whole rhythm section. These records had a raw, exciting sound, often having been recorded in one take, with any mistakes left in. It was a fantastically 'pure' music, sung from the heart with real emotion. Singers

and musicians had to be truly talented, as there was no remixing or electronic gimmickry to help make them sound better.

We knew nothing about these artists, not even what they looked like, so we researched the people to whom these strange names on the records belonged. In books and magazines (there was no quick Google search in those pre-computer days) we found archive pictures of them, and sometimes in these pictures we could see what their fans had looked like, what American teenagers had worn in the 1950s. Way before there were vintage shops and decades before eBay, we tried to dress like the rockabillies. Our early attempts at style were not that successful, but these 1950s rockabilly artists' music was our music. It spoke of life and love, of fast cars, booze, cool young men and sexy women; it was young-teenage-rebellion music and it became the soundtrack to our lives. Every week new recordings or previously unissued material would be unearthed. And – the icing on the cake – we started to contact some of these original, and until then forgotten-about, performers.

The Current Rockin' Scene

Gradually, bands realized that the young kids were becoming a major force, and they started to research more obscure material and to dress and look as if they were onstage in the 1950s; this became known as the 'authentic look' or the 'authentic scene'. 'Dead stock' shoes and clothes (unused and unsold from the 1940s and 1950s) were relatively plentiful if you knew where to look. Valve guitar amps were repaired or reissued and replaced modern electronic units, with Fender and other famous names coming back into the limelight. The upright slap bass was taken up by rockabilly bands, and it has become pretty much the symbol of today's Rockin' music. The authentic Rockin' crowd turned their backs on the modern-sounding bands and their badly mixed, modern-sounding recordings. Old vintage recording equipment is now used once again by bands to record and press real vinyl records that sound loud and bright and a hundred times fuller than the weak, cleaned-up, sterile CDs of today. There is now a huge worldwide market for vintage fashion, and the knock-on effect can be seen in any high-street clothes shop. People talk of 1950s style and fashion making a comeback, but for some of us, they have never been away!

Q. *How many rockabillies does it take to change a lightbulb?*
A. *Ten. One to change it and nine to say they preferred the original.*

As the 1970s crowd grew older and got jobs, they were able to indulge themselves more. The American cars of the late 1940s and early 1950s became more easily attainable, and the hot rods (vehicles modified for extra power and speed) from the era were either imported from America or built in mainland Europe and Scandinavia. The nostalgic car scene in Europe now rivals that of the United States. The other effect of the Rockin' fans' ageing has been the rise of the weekender event and the demise of many small music pubs and clubs. People no longer want to be out in clubs five nights a week, but a few times a year they can go to a festival that caters exclusively for their lifestyle, where they mix with thousands of like-minded people and catch international line-ups that rival anything that happened in the 1950s. It is often said by some of the original artistes that they play to more people at British festivals now than they ever played to at any hall in the United States during the 1950s. And, for a while, it did certainly seem as if America had forgotten its own rockabilly heroes. For the past thirty years most rockabilly gigs, reunions and weekenders have been held in Britain, Scandinavia and the rest of Europe. In the United States, despite the dedicated efforts of some musicians and fans who never gave up the faith, it is only recently that a larger movement has begun to surface.

Current trends on the Rockin' scene include: new young bands playing a mixture of indie music and rockabilly, and recording wild and raw music on independent labels; some of the more established bands playing modern numbers in a rockabilly style; the craze for burlesque, which came from nightclubs, not music shows, but now gets shoehorned in as being from the same era; Rockin' music, original or new, being used in film soundtracks; and appearances by the original performers of the 1950s, who are now in their seventies. In this scene we are used to losing our heroes, but we'll always have their recordings, as fresh, young and rebellious as the day they were laid down in the studio.

Typically, the people who appear in this book, the people on the Rockin' scene, will have more than a passing interest in old music. They will have a passion for the music and the lifestyle. Many people on the scene also have an interest in other aspects of early 1950s style, whether it be fashion or furniture or, of course, cars. Modern life has not been rejected by Rockin' fans, but we choose not to be counted in the mainstream of current trends. We do reject the bland nature of weak,

manufactured pop. It seems a shame to us that, often, talented musicians are not rewarded and that live music has been in such decline. Cheaply produced mass-market clothing with little or no style, and boring cars that no one can tell apart, are not different enough for us. Of course we all own a reliable car for everyday use, and we have microwaves, computers and flat-screen TVs. No one is saying that we want to return to the 1950s. But by enjoying the music and fashion of a stylish era, we can make the current world just slightly more colourful and exciting. We are on the planet only for a short time, and there is no rule that says this time has to be boring!

Inevitably, the people who took part in the Rockin' revival during the late 1970s and the 1980s are now middle-aged – hardly the young rebels they once were. But many of them have had children, some of whom are now discovering the world of rockabilly for themselves. This new generation of rockabillies is

 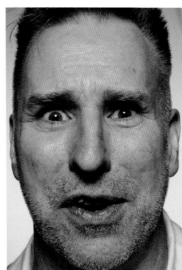 

Jerry Chatabox.

The Caezars at the BBC's recording studio in Maida Vale, London, in 2010, for a performance for Mark Lamarr's God's Jukebox show on BBC Radio 2.

also being fuelled by the current media interest in cool 1950s style and imagery.

New young bands are emerging all the time, and the truly refreshing aspect of this is that they are bringing their own version of rockabilly to the scene. One such band is the Caezars. I first heard about these boys in 2009, when a friend told me that some teenagers were playing at a small indie club in Brighton. To be honest, I didn't have high hopes. I've seen many kids thrashing about on distorted guitars, with little or no discernible talent, all thinking they are the next big thing.

As I stood in the audience, these young guys stepped out on to the stage in sharp 'cat' clothes and introduced themselves. No big attitude, just great-looking kids wanting to entertain. Then they hit the loud pedal and were off; the hairs stood up on the back of my neck, and a wave of excitement passed through the crowd. For the next forty minutes I just stood there smiling and observing the reactions of those around me. Now you must remember that most of the Rockin' crowd have been there, done it, many, many times over; they're a difficult crowd to impress. But suddenly they were all paying attention. This was something special.

The energy and enthusiasm shown by these teenagers brought the music to life. I'd say it was like stepping back in time and seeing a young Rockin' act in the 1950s, except that it was bang up to date. There was nothing retro about these boys. This was their music and it was happening right here, right now. Their style may have been influenced by another era and it was based on the music that I love, but they had made it theirs. They now owned it. It was as modern and relevant to all the teenagers in the audience as any other popular music being produced today.

The Caezars performed a mix of garage, punk and rockabilly, and delivered it with more energy than was frankly decent! And the pack of teen fans jammed down the front screamed their approval. The future of the Rockin' scene? It's already here.

If you are intrigued by the images in this book, get yourself down to one of the many great Rockin' events (some are listed on page 192). Listen to the music, with its infectious energy, and watch the incredible dancing. It may just make you tap your foot. It may just make you smile. Or it may totally change your life, as it has done for thousands of Rockin' fans around the world.

Jerry Chatabox, November 2010

THE ROOTS OF ROCKABILLY

I wanted to find out a little about rockabilly's origins and how it's doing now, and to do this I had to go to America's southern states, the home of rockabilly. There are two names that, to my mind, represent the foundation of rockabilly music: Hank Williams and Carl Perkins. Both men came from the South (Hank from Alabama and Carl from Tennessee), and both had very humble beginnings; both were from conservative, religious backgrounds; and both were taught to play the guitar by local bluesmen. I wanted to try to understand a little of where they came from, via the landscapes in which they were raised and the towns that held them for a while. I also wanted to discover how rockabilly is getting on in the South, and if it's still relevant today. This meant I had to go on a bit of a road trip, taking in some 2000 miles of American heartland. I wanted to follow Hank first, so I began in Alabama.

Hank Williams (1923–1953)

Hank was born in Mount Olive, Alabama, and the road leading to the Mount Olive West Baptist Church is now called Hank Williams Road. I am quite apprehensive, and also a little excited, as I look for the church. Hank sang gospel here as a boy, so I was expecting a bit of a fanfare when the church appeared, but there is no reference to Hank apart from the road name. The church sits on open ground, with a few small gravestones dotted about. It's plain and obviously still in working order, but I'm a bit disappointed, to be honest. Given that Hank was one of America's greatest songwriters, I had imagined that there would be something more. However, on reflection, I'm pleased that the chapel looked as it did. It is, after all, a place of worship.

I decide to head a few miles up the road to Georgiana, Hank's home for a few years during his youth. So far the landscape has been relentlessly flat and unchanging, and the oppressive 100°F (38°C) heat is very draining after a while. There are churches everywhere, and their

Hank Williams immortalized on a Ford.

Opposite, top: Mount Olive West Baptist Church, on Hank Williams Road, near Georgiana, Alabama. Hank sang at the church as a boy.

Opposite, bottom: Georgiana's Ga-ana Theatre, where Hank Williams and the Drifting Cowboys played in the late 1930s and early 1940s.

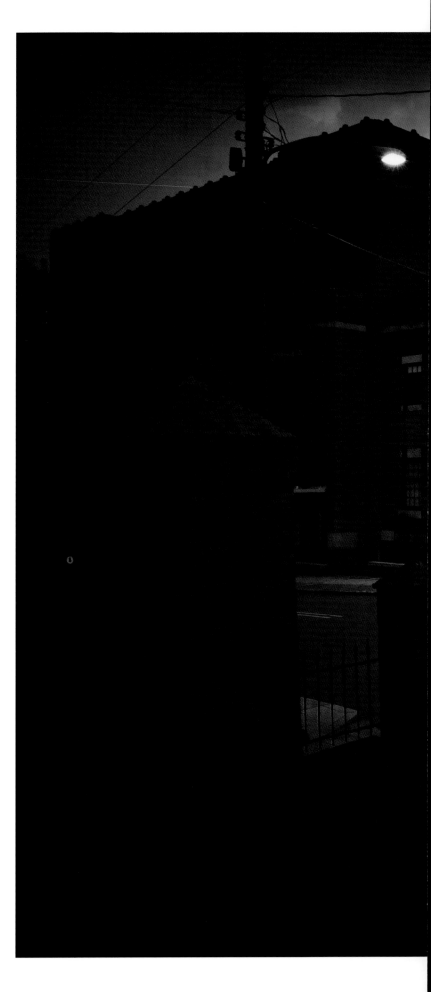

number seems wholly out of proportion to their
surroundings and the apparently small number of
people. And Alabama has a lot of poverty. It's plain to
see, nowhere more so than in Georgiana. Main Street,
which has a railroad running right through it, is
deserted. The shops are boarded up or simply empty.
One or two are struggling to survive, but the feeling I get
is one of desperation. There is, however, a music venue
that stands on Main Street. It's called the Ga-ana Theatre
and is a place in which Hank performed with his band,
the Drifting Cowboys, when he was sixteen. Georgiana
is also home to the Hank Williams Boyhood Home &
Museum, situated in the house in which he lived for a
few years. It's closed when I get there, but I'm not too
annoyed because my aim is to photograph not the tourist
venues but the streets and landscapes with which Hank
lived and that influenced him.

This leads me to a location mentioned in one of my
favourite of Hank's songs, 'Lost Highway'. This highway
has been identified by the local town as the I-65, but that
wasn't around in Hank's day. It is more likely that the
I-31, between Georgiana and Greenville, is a better
representation. I travel up and down it for a while, trying
to get a feel for it, and decide that it has probably not
changed very much.

There isn't a great deal of traffic, so for a while I
feel I'm in a good place to live, as Hank did. He would
have travelled from Georgiana to Shreveport, Louisiana,
some seven hours' drive away, to perform on the *Louisiana
Hayride*, an extremely popular radio and television show
during its 1950s heyday. (Shreveport, which I drove to
a few days later, is, and I think always has been, an
entertainment city. It appears to be a destination for
gamblers. The auditorium that held the *Hayride* is a
1930s beauty; it was closed when I tried to visit it, and
the area around it was deserted, but I could really get
a feeling for how special this place would have been
at the time.)

Opposite: Hank Williams's 'Lost Highway'? The I-31 between Georgiana and Greenville, Alabama (top); Tiptonville, Tennessee, birthplace and boyhood home of Carl Perkins (bottom).

Singer Tab Hawkins's guitar, with Carl Perkins's signature (upside down under the metal plate).

I move on north-east from Greenville up the I-31 to Montgomery, Alabama's capital. Hank lived here with his extremely attractive wife, Audrey, and the city is now the site of the 'official' Hank Williams Museum. The museum is excellent, and houses the famous baby-blue Cadillac in which Hank died. Taking photographs is not allowed, but that's OK; I get a sense of the man. Hank was very tall and slim, and was slightly stooped (it is thought he had a mild case of spina bifida). He dressed extravagantly, and the flamboyantly embroidered Nudie suits, by the tailor Nudie Cohn, are amazing. It's clear that Hank has had a huge influence not only on country music, but also on all popular music; in his short musical life he wrote some 225 songs. His lyrics were harsh and brutal for the time, full of pain and loss, and there is an honesty in his words that people could connect with and understand.

The trip so far has taken me through a number of southern states. Constant throughout have been the cotton fields and the churches (as they were in Hank's day), the pickup trucks, the 'Gas–Food–Lodging' opportunities along the highway and the overriding sense of being at the heart of America's blue-collar homeland.

Carl Perkins (1932–1998)

Carl Perkins was born and raised in Tiptonville, Tennessee, about two hours' drive north of Memphis. Tiptonville's Carl Perkins Visitor Center maintains his early home, a very small, humble wooden house that was closed when I was in town. My drive around Tiptonville reveals another area of relative poverty, and churches and cotton fields are, as always, everywhere. In fact, the cotton crop is being picked and there are a number of stubble fires burning. The vast Mississippi River passes just outside Tiptonville, so I walk down to the water's edge; I imagine that this is something Carl did in his youth, and that he was as awed as I was by the river's brooding menace and its natural beauty. Tiptonville's other large

The vast Mississippi River, on the edge of Tiptonville,
Tennessee.

body of water is Reelfoot Lake (much of it swamp-like), formed by a series of earthquakes in 1811 and 1812. The cypress trees that grow around and even in the water make me feel that I really am in the rural South.

On the streets of Tiptonville stray 'lumps' of cotton eddy among the buildings. Many of these structures are derelict, and one gets the sense of an industry in decline, or at least one that has been transformed by modern agricultural methods. By the railroad is a strange-looking, small, isolated building, a liquor store into which I go to buy 'provisions'. The lady who works there tells me that the store was built in the early 1930s and hasn't changed much since then ... and I believe her.

I learn that the following day the Blue Bank fishing and hunting resort, by Reelfoot Lake, will be holding the Roundhouse Reunion – a daytime event celebrating a small local venue that in the 1940s and 1950s was home to a jukebox popular with the town's more youthful souls. Carl certainly went there, and even played there. Tab Hawkins, a singer who knew Carl well, confirms this when I meet him at the event the next day, and has his precious old Lyle guitar signed by Carl. The reunion is a sedate affair, with the performers playing a variety of country, rock 'n' roll and rockabilly from the deck of a lorry, and the sound isn't very good. The open-sided roundhouse, which is not the original building but sits on the same site, acts as a dance floor and is thronged by people who danced to the jukebox sixty years ago. The rest of the crowd have brought picnics, coolers and chairs, and spend a few hours listening to the music and basking in the sun.

Carl left Tiptonville and made nearby Jackson his home for many years. Jackson is where an old colleague of Carl, Henry Harrison, runs the Rockabilly Hall of Fame, which holds Friday-night gigs to celebrate the music. I attend one of these evenings, and here too the audience are of a certain age, and they are very helpful and interested in my project. I ask if in Jackson there is

any interest in rockabilly among the younger crowd, and am told that there isn't much interest in anything apart from trying to make a living. The town is deserted, and although the centre is pleasant enough, containing a number of good examples of early twentieth-century buildings, there is a ghost-town feel that I have experienced many times on my travels in the South so far.

The house band plays a number of covers, and a series of singers in the audience get a chance to do their thing on stage – some of them quite well. There is a lively crowd on the dance floor, and later in the evening a group of students from the Union Baptist college arrive to join in the fun. The band's drummer, Bobby Cash, who recorded at Sun Studio with rockabilly singer and guitarist Kenny Parchman in the 1950s, tells me that about ten miles out of Jackson is a venue, the Pine Ridge Club, that was around in those days.

I take a trip out there the next morning, and, sure enough, there stands the club among the pine trees. Like many bars and clubs in this part of the United States, the place has no windows and as a result looks a little unwelcoming; there is a pickup with a flat tyre outside, and empty beer bottles are littered all about. As I am photographing the venue a pickup pulls up, and the driver turns out to be the grandson of the man who built the club. I ask what kind of music is performed here now, and he tells me that it's mostly country and a bit of rock 'n' roll; apparently, it used to be a popular rockabilly venue and Carl Perkins performed here.

Carl made his name at Sun Studio, a short drive away in Memphis. The studio, which is in a slightly bohemian area east of downtown, is still in operation, and Memphis is still a big music town. Most of the building's interior is designed for tourists, with a museum, diner and gift shop, but the recording studio itself is pretty much in its original condition. There is definitely an atmosphere in the recording studio, and I feel quite honoured when I am allowed to be alone there while I make my pictures.

Sun Studio, Memphis, Tennessee. The (still used)
recording studio is pretty much in its original 1950s state.

One of the Friday-night gigs at the Rockabilly Hall
of Fame, Jackson, Tennessee.

Some very worn gaffer-tape marks on the floor show where Elvis Presley, his bass player, Bill Black, and his guitarist, Scotty Moore, stood while recording, and the original Shure 55 microphone used by Carl Perkins, Elvis, Howlin' Wolf and many others still stands. For most people the studio is associated with Elvis, but Jayne White, a Sun Studio tour guide and a fount of knowledge on all things rockabilly, is good enough to say that Carl has been a little overlooked as a creator and is worthy of the title 'King of Rockabilly'. In my view, his music from his Sun Studio days is about as 'pure' as rockabilly gets.

I ask Jayne if she thinks that rockabilly is a lively scene in Memphis, and she replies candidly that the scene is no longer popular here and that the only rockabilly in Memphis is to be heard at tourist-trap shrimp-and-steak diners. When I tell her that the scene is thriving in Britain and Europe, she replies that everyone does Americana well, except Americans.

I've travelled nearly two thousand miles through the southern United States and have discovered that the home of rockabilly no longer loves rockabilly. Jackson's Rockabilly Hall of Fame exists only as a labour of love, and we have to thank Henry Harrison for keeping it running; Sun Studio is a great place and I recommend a visit, but it's really a shrine to Elvis and to Sam Phillips, who founded the studio and the Sun Records label in the early 1950s; and although Hank Williams is honoured in Montgomery, his influence on rockabilly music is not really recognized and he is regarded, quite fairly, as one of the greats of country music. Wherever I travelled in the South, the people who loved rockabilly originally were still celebrating it today; but today's Rockin' scene has moved largely to the West Coast, where rockabilly is played and recorded with a Mexican flag attached to it.

THE ROCKIN' SCENE

For a long time, I had been scouting out ideas for an absorbing photographic project that I could build into a book. After the success of my previous book, *Hells Angels Motorcycle Club* (2004), my publisher wanted something new from me, and all my friends were asking me what I was going to do next, but I was not sure where to go. I'd had a look at a few subcultures that had interested me in the past, but soon discovered that these were either impossible to access, not as interesting as I originally thought or simply too dangerous. One day a friend said to me, rather quietly, 'Rockabilly'. I'd heard about it: it was something that happened a long time ago, then sort of reappeared in the 1970s or 1980s, but, as far as I knew, was now lost to another time. I decided to check it out.

Rockabilly Rave UK 2009, Pontins Holiday Park, Camber Sands, East Sussex

I arrive at Pontins in Camber Sands the day before the five-day Rockabilly Rave begins. Not many people are about, but I'm due to meet a gentleman called Jerry Chatabox; apparently, he is 'the man' when it comes to all things rockabilly, and he has organized the Rave since 1997. While wandering about outside the site before our meeting, I spot a very smart-looking pickup in the car park and I take a few shots of it. Then this guy wearing turn-ups appears and says hello; he tells me he owns the car, so I ask him a question about it. Big mistake: forty minutes later I have the answer to my question, but my head hurts a bit (I'm not that interested in cars, and asked him the question only to be polite, as I was photographing his car). The guy appears to be satisfied that he has told me absolutely everything he possibly could in answer to my question, and wanders off to chat to owners of the now rapidly arriving posse of 1950s vehicles. Apart from the occasional Humber, most of the cars are American.

Then I meet Jerry. He looks the rockabilly part and is a bundle of energy, moving along at a good speed and

rarely ceasing to talk and crack 'jokes' that he thinks are funny. He says I can do what I want at the Rave, gives me 'triple A' and I'm up and running. I'm at the Rave with cameras and lights, but am not really sure what to expect …

Some 2500 people turned up to the Rave. Pontins must have done some good business: rumour had it that they ran out of beer (these rockabilly people really do drink a lot). At Pontins the bedrooms are not very comfortable and the bathrooms retain their original 1950s design and finish. But, as I learn over the Rave weekend, the Rockin' scene is all about the clothes, the cars and the music, and having a really good time – most of which (apart from impromptu gigs and private parties) take place away from the accommodation. Over the course of the weekend I take quite a number of pictures and meet some great people from around the world, and learn something about the scene. Everybody attending the Rave looks fantastic, even when wearing simply a T-shirt, jeans and All Stars. Everyone seems to know everybody else and it's all very friendly. Outsiders are welcomed, which makes my work quite easy. There's no stress here; people just socialize, shop at the stalls selling original gear, and get ready for the evening's entertainment.

It's the music that attracts so many here. There are DJs plying their trade on two separate stages. Some people prefer the gruelling downstairs bar, where it's crowded and sweaty and impossible to take photographs. There's a bit more room upstairs in the main ballroom, and this is where the live bands play. Jerry books bands from around the world for the Rave. Some of the headliners here were recording in the 1950s, so it must come as a bit of a surprise for them to receive an invitation to perform in the UK some fifty years later. It's in the ballroom that I witness some fantastic dancing; the slick moves, evident passion and love of the music are all around. I have no ability whatsoever to dance, but

the enthusiasm generated by the scene and the music is infectious. I dare not dance in public, so, backstage, in between shooting portraits, I take full advantage of the acres of space. It's not pretty, but I have great fun.

The people attending the Rave are up for a discussion at all times, and I keep asking them 'What is rockabilly? What's the essence and heart of the scene?' Well, the Rockin' scene could be described as quite insular. There is a feeling of ownership, as can be found in most small, like-minded groups of people or clubs. Nearly everyone is more than happy to chat with me, an outsider, but I get the sense that I am being sized up to gauge whether or not I am a genuine fan or, as my assistant, Lex, put it, a scene licker: someone who jumps into a fashion, buys all the gear and pretends to be an authority on the subject, then moves on a year later to the next on the list of scenes in which to be seen and involved.

The other thing I notice is that there isn't really a consensus on what is and what is not rockabilly music. It's a discussion I have time and again. Some people are very laid-back about the question, but others are purists. Some enjoy Elvis Presley, for example, and consider him to be integral to the Rockin' scene, while others view him as insincere and as someone who left rockabilly in pursuit of the filthy dollar. (Hank Williams and Carl Perkins are seen as the pioneers of the rockabilly genre.) The music is taken very seriously: if an individual doesn't consider a track being played by a DJ to be 'pure', he or she will walk right up to the DJ and give him (or her) grief about it. Similarly, the introduction of burlesque to some of the weekend events has divided opinion. Yes, burlesque was a phenomenon of the 1950s, but it wasn't part of any 'hayride' or Rockin' event back then. However, many in the scene see burlesque not as stripping as such, but more as a respectful tease.

Generally, people are pretty forgiving of those who are new to the scene. I also photographed at the Rhythm

Riot, another weekender, where rockabilly and R&B sit side by side. Some of the dancing and clothing there would not be considered pure rockabilly, but I thought everyone looked great.

When it comes to cars of the era, the purists get very stringent. As someone who knows little more about cars than where to point them, I found discussions I overheard or mistakenly got involved in quite mystifying. I recall once admiring a Cadillac (yes, it was pink) within earshot of someone who is totally into the Rockin' scene. His withering look suggested that I might have something wrong in the head; it turned out the car was a 1960s model, not a 1950s one. Having said that, some of the cars I saw and photographed at the Rave were absolutely beautiful. The time and effort (and quite a bit of cash) that had been invested in them was to be respected.

The Dancing

For me, the dancing was the most exciting part of the Rockin' scene. Whenever I visited an event, be it a gig or a weekender, there was always the movement in unison of well-dressed bodies. My first experience of a rockabilly dance floor in full motion was breathtaking. As the DJ put on a record, it was evident almost immediately that this was one for the ladies. A sea of females took to the floor and did the Stroll in perfect synchronization. (The Stroll is very much like line dancing, with each participant bringing their own slight variation to a particular set of moves.) It was as if the display had been rehearsed, but, as I was to learn, it was nothing exceptional. Meanwhile, the guys stood on the side and watched. Next up was the Bop, an opportunity for the men to show off and try to catch someone's eye. Then they all came together for the Jive.

There is no hint of predatory intentions at these gigs. The women want to dance and the guys realize that, so don't hassle them. There is a real sense of good manners and respect on the dance floor.

The Clothes

Rockabilly was, and still is, about smart clothes. Whatever the time of day or night, you would be hard-pressed to find a scruffy rockabilly – a drunk one, certainly, but not a scruffy one. The music came from a cross between blues and hillbilly, and the clothes reflect the music's origins and the period. The hillbilly dress code was not well thought of back in the day, so the only real reference now to the hillbilly look is the turn-up.

The Rave offers people the chance to dress up, although I got the sense that they dress in the same style outside these events, too. The women wear what I can describe only as 'proper' dresses in the evening, with their hair teased to within an inch of its life, while the men, if not wearing a suit, make sure that their hair is clean and combed back, their shirt is pressed and their jeans are sharp. Although many people outside the scene see this style of clothing as outlandish, I saw quite a bit of conservatism in it.

There are those who will, if they can afford it, invest in anything that is authentic. It can cost as much as £1000 for a vintage gaberdine shirt, and up to £3000 for an original pair of selvedge Levi's from the 1950s. Such prized brands as Shaheen, Nudie, Turk and Chimayo will send some people into a frenzy of spending.

Rockabilly Rave USA 2009, Orleans Hotel & Casino, Las Vegas, Nevada

It is with a feeling of dread and queasiness that I arrive in Las Vegas (I'd been to Vegas a few times before for work, and had never enjoyed the town). The Rave USA – only the second to be held in the United States – is to take place at a hotel off the strip, which means that the place will be average at best and, like everything here, huge. I have an invitation to a pre-Rave party at the Thunderbird Lounge at the Aruba Hotel. There I find the beating heart of the Los Angeles rockabilly scene in the form of musicians from Wild Records, who are performing at the

Rockabilly Rave UK, Camber Sands, East Sussex.

party's show. (There is a fast-growing scene in LA and along the West Coast generally, with a young Mexican population who have taken the rockabilly sound and given it their own touch of Latino energy.)

During the show the crowd of like-minded types throw themselves into each performance with such force and physicality that I fear for someone's life. In this tiny, stage-less venue, throughout their performance the musicians are offered beer by the dancers (which they accept) and are constantly being jostled by the crowd, but they seem to accept it as the norm. There is a power and energy in the room that transports people to another place.

I take this energy back to the Rave the next day, and although there is a good vibe there, because of the huge size of the venue the atmosphere doesn't match that at the Thunderbird Lounge. Walking from my hotel bedroom through the vast ground-floor casino, populated by dead-eyed people leaning on one-armed bandits, and then entering a ballroom full of well-dressed and perfectly presented 'weirdos' is a strange experience, the memory of which will stay with me for some time.

Hot Rod Hayride 2009, Bisley Shooting Ground, Surrey

The Rockabilly Rave is about the music. The Hot Rod Hayride (a three-day weekender that has been held since 2005) is definitely more about the cars. Bisley is a strange place. I once shot there (with a camera) for a magazine, and wandered among the many clubhouses, soaking up the slightly elitist atmosphere. On this occasion, the arrival of a slick of rockabillies put paid to any sense of middle-class self-satisfaction. With cars from another era all about, noisy and bright, I was put in mind of the film *American Graffiti* (1973). The guys are here to check out one another's cars (is every nut and bolt original?), to listen to the bands and, of course, to drink the place dry. Among the 1500 or so people attending I recognize a few

faces from the Rave. The differences at this event are but a few. Apart from the cars, the main difference is that this time everybody is camping; conditions are basic even compared to Pontins, yet people manage to appear perfectly groomed as they emerge from a two-person ridge tent that cost twenty quid at the local garage.

In some ways, the Rockin' scene seems to reflect the moral codes of the 1950s. There is certainly a mutual respect among those in the scene, which they extend to people outside of it. There is also a genuine politeness in the way they engage with people, and they take real pride in their appearance. I hear from some people in the scene that, outside of scene events, they are treated as if they were slightly freakish, merely because of their hairstyles and clothes. It's depressing to think that we live in a country where people are judged on what they wear. But those who love this scene are pretty straight-talking, and no doubt deal with this idiocy in their own charming way. It was a true pleasure to meet everyone I encountered, and I really enjoyed spending time with them. I am none the wiser about what is and what isn't rockabilly, and will no doubt be hauled over the coals for including images in this book that are not 'pure'. But as that discussion rages on among those who have been in the scene far longer than me, I feel that I have captured just a little of what the life of someone in the Rockin' scene is about.

Pages 36–37: Cruise to Dungeness, Kent, Rockabilly Rave UK.

Rockabilly Rave UK, Camber Sands, East Sussex (opposite); Hot Rod Hayride, Bisley, Surrey (below).

Motorcycle detail, Rockabilly Rave UK, Camber Sands,
East Sussex (opposite); Scavengers weekender, Stelling
Minnis, Kent (below).

Overleaf: Hot Rod Hayride, Bisley, Surrey.

Rockabilly Rave UK, Camber Sands, East Sussex.

Clarke, singer with Moonshine Reunion (below), and
a driver in his car, Hot Rod Hayride, Bisley, Surrey.

Robert Williams (aka Big Sandy), Rockabilly Rave
USA, Las Vegas.

Rockabilly Rave UK, Camber Sands, East Sussex.

Big Jay McNeely, Rhythm Riot, Camber Sands, East Sussex (left); John Lewis, singer, Rockabilly Rave USA, Las Vegas (opposite).

Deke Dickerson, Rockabilly Rave UK, Camber Sands,
East Sussex (opposite); Ash, guitarist, Rhythm Riot,
Camber Sands, East Sussex (above).

Knocksville band members, Sin City, Koko club,
Camden, north London.

Tribute to Janis Martin ('the female Elvis'): (left to right) Rockin Bonnie, Jessie, Little Esther, Maibell, Miss Mary Ann and Lynette Morgan. Rockabilly Rave UK, Camber Sands, East Sussex.

Overleaf: AJ, singer with the Caezars, Bedford Arms pub, Balham, south London.

*Mark (opposite) and 'Lucky' Phil (right), Rockabilly
Rave UK, Camber Sands, East Sussex.*

Miss Mary Ann and Little Esther, Rockabilly Rave USA,
Las Vegas (opposite); cruise to Lydd, Kent, Rockabilly
Rave UK (below).

Brighton Rumble at the Engine Room, Brighton (left and below); Rockabilly Rave USA, Las Vegas (opposite).

Hot Rod Hayride, Bisley, Surrey.

Santos, singer, Nightingale Studios, Burbank, California.

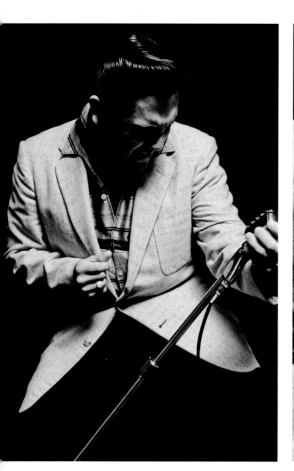

Pages 74–75: Rockabilly Rave UK, Camber Sands, East Sussex.

King Kukulele, Rockabilly Rave UK, Camber Sands,
East Sussex (below); Crazy Joe, Rockabilly Rave USA,
Las Vegas (opposite).

Rockabilly Rave UK, Camber Sands, East Sussex (below);
Toni, Rockabilly Rave UK (opposite).

Pages 82–83: Rockabilly Rave UK, Camber Sands,
East Sussex.

Joey Simeone of the
Bellfuries (opposite) and
Ian Agar of the Infernos
(right), Rockabilly Rave
UK, Camber Sands,
East Sussex.

Rhythm Riot, Camber Sands, East Sussex.

Rockabilly Rave UK, Camber Sands, East Sussex.

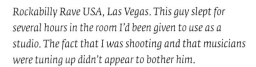

Rockabilly Rave USA, Las Vegas. This guy slept for several hours in the room I'd been given to use as a studio. The fact that I was shooting and that musicians were tuning up didn't appear to bother him.

Johnny Kidd (opposite) and Del Villareal, Rockin' DJ and MC (right), Rockabilly Rave UK, Camber Sands, East Sussex.

Overleaf: Rhythm Riot, Camber Sands, East Sussex.

Larry and Lorrie Collins (the Collins Kids),
Rockabilly Rave USA, Las Vegas.

Left to right: Crazy Joe, Larry Collins, Joe Sixpack and Deke Dickerson, all playing double-necked Mosrites, Rockabilly Rave USA, Las Vegas.

Luis of the Wildfires, Nightingale Studios, Burbank,
California (below); Rockabilly Rave UK, Camber
Sands, East Sussex (opposite).

Pages 100–101: Rockabilly Rave UK, Camber Sands,
East Sussex.

The Stroll in action, Sin City, Koko club, Camden, north London (opposite); Rockabilly Rave UK, Camber Sands, East Sussex (below).

Bobby Trimble, demon drummer, Rockabilly Rave UK,
Camber Sands, East Sussex (below); Paul Ansell,
singer, Hot Rod Hayride, Bisley, Surrey (opposite).

Sylvain, Rockabilly Rave UK, Camber Sands, East
Sussex (above); one of a number of impromptu gigs that
take place at the Rave (above, right).

Malcolm, Detonators CC Sunday meet, south London (opposite); Hot Rod Hayride, Bisley, Surrey (right): these nervous-looking gentlemen were about to compete in the Soapbox Derby, which requires entrants to construct their own engineless vehicles and then race against the clock down a slight hill.

'It's not the clothes or the cars. It's if you have it in your heart ... that's what matters.'

Robbie, on what the Rockin' scene is all about

The Doc (above) and Tennessee (above, right),
Hastings; Robbie, Hot Rot Hayride, Bisley, Surrey
(opposite).

Rockabilly Rave UK, Camber Sands, East Sussex
(opposite); Hot Rod Hayride, Bisley, Surrey (below).

Rosie, Rockabilly Rave UK, Camber Sands, East Sussex (below); Scavengers weekender, Stelling Minnis, Kent (below, right).

Rhythm Riot, Camber Sands, East Sussex.

*The Memphis Flyers and audience, Cinque Ports pub,
Rye, East Sussex.*

Hot Rod Hayride, Bisley, Surrey (below); Cristhie, Rockabilly Rave UK, Camber Sands, East Sussex (opposite).

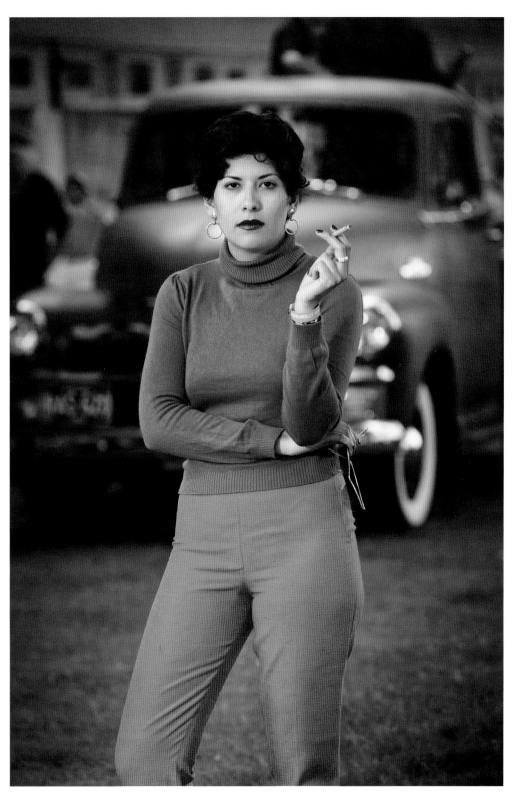

Rob's Chop Shop,
Rockabilly Rave UK,
Camber Sands, East Sussex
(opposite); Carlos Gomez
at work at Hawleywood's
barber shop and shaving
parlour, Long Beach,
California (right).

The Queen Vic pub at Pontins, Camber Sands, East Sussex, during the Rockabilly Rave UK.

Wayne, Rockabilly Rave UK, Camber Sands, East Sussex (opposite); Rockabilly Rave UK (above), and the cruise to Dungeness, Kent (above, centre); Scavengers weekender, Stelling Minnis, Kent (above, right).

Hot Rod Hayride, Bisley, Surrey (below); Blip Blop, DJ,
Rockabilly Rave UK, Camber Sands, East Sussex (opposite).

Brigitte and Jeanette (left), Ellie May and Jo (opposite), Rockabilly Rave UK, Camber Sands, East Sussex.

Cruise to Lydd, Kent, Rockabilly Rave UK (below);
Kitty Katastrophe (opposite, left) and Ursula Undress,
Sin City, Koko club, Camden, north London.

Hot Rod Hayride, Bisley, Surrey (previous page, below and opposite).

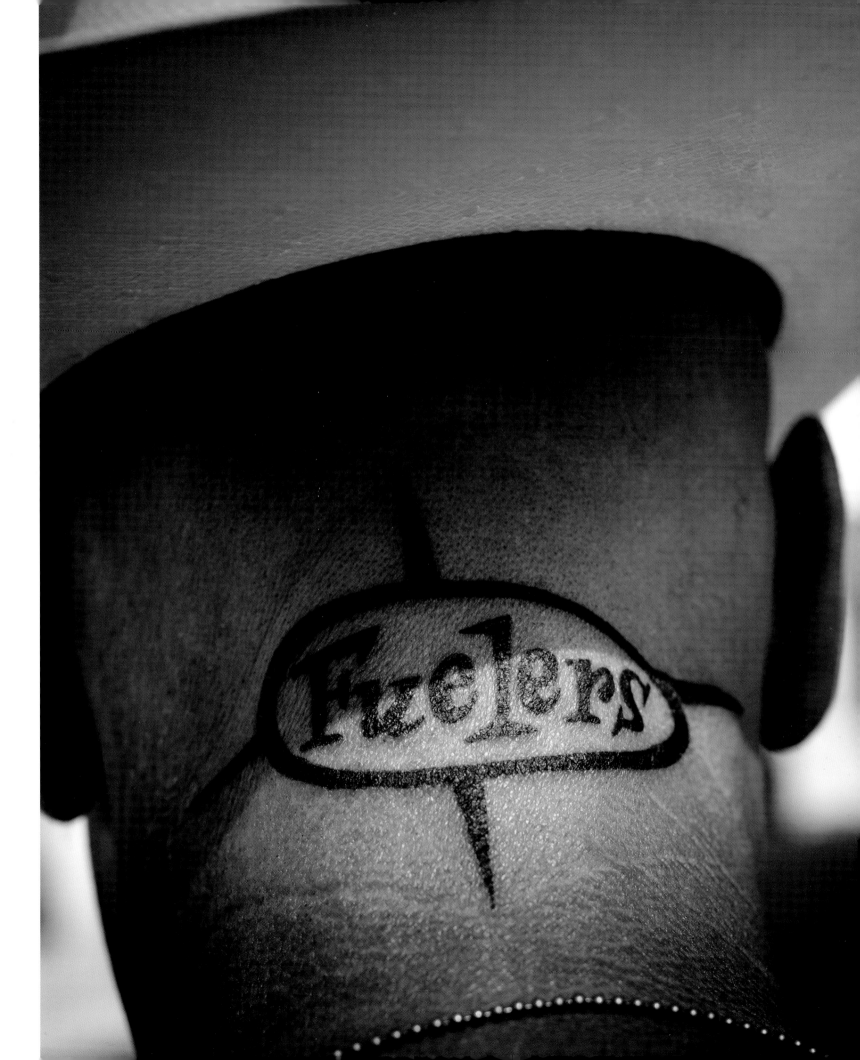

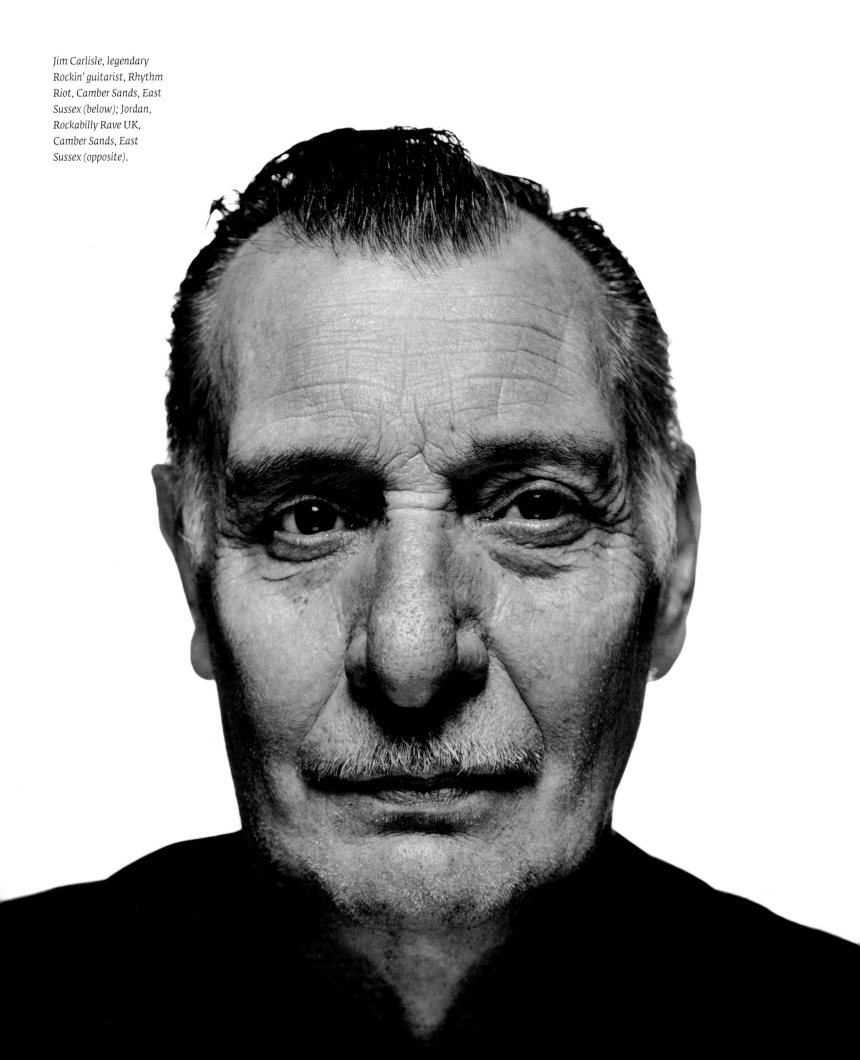

Jim Carlisle, legendary Rockin' guitarist, Rhythm Riot, Camber Sands, East Sussex (below); Jordan, Rockabilly Rave UK, Camber Sands, East Sussex (opposite).

Cruise to Dungeness, Kent, Rockabilly Rave UK
(opposite); Hot Rod Hayride, Bisley, Surrey (below).

Madame Butterfly in her tattoo parlour in Hastings,
East Sussex (above); Rockabilly Rave UK, Camber
Sands, East Sussex (above, right).

Left to right: Niko, Brian, Dirk and DJ Go!, Rockabilly Rave UK, Camber Sands, East Sussex.

Rockabilly Rave UK, Camber Sands, East Sussex
(below); Big Ed at Big Ed's Record Shop, Long Beach,
California (opposite).

Lucky Marcel (opposite) and Miss Ruby Ann (right), Rockabilly Rave UK, Camber Sands, East Sussex.

Rockabilly Rave USA, Las Vegas (opposite); 'Sugar Balls', drummer (below), and Ronnie of the Fleabops (below, right), Rockabilly Rave USA.

Sage, singer with the
Lucky Stars (left), and
some of the crowd at
Rockabilly Rave USA,
Las Vegas (opposite).

Miss Honey Lulu, Hot Rod Hayride, Bisley, Surrey (opposite); Missy Malone, Rhythm Riot, Camber Sands, East Sussex (right).

The Ragtime Wranglers' Jelle (aka Joe Sixpack;
below), Huib (aka Huey Moor; opposite, left) and
'Sexy' Sietse (opposite, right), Rhythm Riot, Camber
Sands, East Sussex.

'We shook the devil loose! We bopped those blues! It's uptempo, it's rhythm. You ain't sitting there worrying about car payments or house notes. You're out there shakin' dust loose on those honky-tonk floors.'

Carl Perkins

Rockabilly Rave UK, Camber Sands, East Sussex
(below); Lady Marmalade, Sin City, Koko club,
Camden, north London (opposite).

Miss Dolly Blow-Up (opposite) and Chrys Columbine
(right), Rhythm Riot, Camber Sands, East Sussex.

Overleaf: Outside the Thunderbird Lounge at the
Aruba Hotel, Las Vegas, at the pre-Rave party for
the Rockabilly Rave USA.

'You're either in it or you're not ...
It's a black-and-white thing.'

Alex, on the Rockin' scene

Alex, Rockabilly Rave USA, Las Vegas (opposite);
Rockabilly Rave UK, Camber Sands, East Sussex (above).

Jessie and the Orbits, Sin City, Koko club, Camden,
north London.

Rockabilly Rave UK, Camber Sands, East Sussex
(below); Wayne 'the Train' Hancock, Rockabilly
Rave UK (opposite).

'Man, I'm like a stab wound in the fabric
of country music in Nashville. See that
bloodstain slowly spreading? That's me.'

Wayne 'the Train' Hancock
(the Viper of Melody)

Jimmy Dell, singer (opposite), and Gaultier, guitarist (right), Rockabilly Rave UK, Camber Sands, East Sussex.

Scotty (opposite), and action on the dance floor (below),
Rockabilly Rave UK, Camber Sands, East Sussex.

Crazy Joe and Deke Dickerson, Rockabilly Rave UK, Camber Sands, East Sussex (left); Rockabilly Rave USA, Las Vegas (opposite).

Pages 186–87: Detonators CC, south London.

Rocky Burnette, Rockabilly Rave USA, Las Vegas (below); DJ Smokey Joe, Rockabilly Rave UK, Camber Sands, East Sussex (opposite).

Pages 190–91: The Caezars recording at the BBC's studio in Maida Vale, London, in 2010 for Mark Lamarr's God's Jukebox *show on BBC Radio 2.*

ROCKIN' EVENTS

UNITED KINGDOM

Hemsby Rock 'n' Roll
May; Hemsby, Norfolk
hemsbyrocknroll.co.uk

Rockabilly Rave UK
June; Camber Sands, East Sussex
rockabillyrave.co.uk

Hot Rod Hayride
July/August; Bisley, Surrey
hotrodhayride.com

Rhythm Riot
November; Camber Sands, East Sussex
rhythmriot.com

UNITED STATES

Viva Las Vegas
April; Las Vegas, Nevada
vivalasvegas.net/vlv14/

AUSTRALIA

Wintersun Festival
May/June; Port Macquarie, New South Wales
wintersun.org.au

BELGIUM

Rockin' Around Turnhout
April; Turnhout, Antwerp
rockinaroundturnhout.be

CROATIA

Tear It Up
June; Medulin, northern Croatia
tearitupfestival.net

GERMANY

Let's Get Wild
December; Stuttgart
myspace.com/letsgetwildnewyearsparty

ITALY

Summer Jamboree
July/August; Senigallia, Ancora
summerjamboree.com

SPAIN

High Rock-A-Billy
September; Calafell, Tarragona
myspace.com/highrockabilly

SWEDEN

A-Bombers Old-Style Weekend
July/August; Backamo Lägerplatz, south
of Uddevalla, west coast of Sweden
a-bombers.com

This book is dedicated to Martha.

ACKNOWLEDGEMENTS

I'd like to thank Lex Kembery for his generous assistance, his huge enthusiasm and his unending knowledge. His company while I made this book and his enduring friendship are invaluable to me.

I'd also like to thank the legend that is Jerry Chatabox, who let me into the scene and helped me with advice, access and contacts. His contribution to this book adds a dimension of knowledge and integrity that comes only from someone who has been in the Rockin' scene for as long as he has.

And, of course, I would also like to say thanks to Ros, who puts up with me and gives me so much support.

My thanks also go to the following (in no particular order): Woody, Madame Butterfly, Miss Mary Ann, Anya, Tom Ingram, Reb Kennedy, Smokey Joe, Robin and Colette from the Rythm Riot, the Executioners CC, the Scavengers, the Detonators CC, Alex Tapia, Randy Festejo, Chris Schorr and Jayne White at Sun Studio, Mick Geary, Langley and Penny Gifford, Dave Mumbles, Henry Harrison, Hugh Merrell, Nicola Bailey, Claire Chandler, Marion Moisy, Alenka Oblak and all at Merrell. To everybody who let me take their photograph, thank you all for helping out and giving your time.

Andrew Shaylor, December 2010

First published 2011 by

Merrell Publishers Limited
81 Southwark Street
London SE1 0HX

merrellpublishers.com

Main texts, captions and illustrations
     copyright © 2011 Andrew Shaylor
Foreword copyright © 2011 Jerry Chatabox
Design and layout copyright © 2011 Merrell
     Publishers Limited

British Library Cataloguing-in-Publication Data:
Shaylor, Andrew.
     Rockin' : the rockabilly scene.
     1. Rockabilly music–Pictorial works.
     2. Rockabilly music–History and criticism.
     I. Title
     779.9'78166'092-dc22

ISBN 978-1-8589-4528-6

Produced by Merrell Publishers Limited
Designed by Nicola Bailey
Project-managed by Marion Moisy

Printed and bound in China

FRONT JACKET: *Rockabilly Rave UK, Camber Sands, East Sussex.*
BACK JACKET: *Wild Records pre-Rave party, Thunderbird Lounge, Aruba Hotel, Las Vegas.*
PAGE 1: *Sun Studio's early 1950s Shure 55 microphone, used by Carl Perkins.*
PAGES 4–5: *Toad, Scavengers weekender, Stelling Minnis, Kent.*
PAGE 6: *Hayden, Rockabilly Rave USA, Las Vegas.*
PAGE 8: *Rockabilly Rave UK, Camber Sands, East Sussex.*

SAGE
Division of Sage & Sand · Hollywood 28

45-261b
Time 1:53

Sage & Sand Music
Pub. SESAC

LOVE, COME BACK TO ME
(Oscar Patton)
JIMMY PATTON
Piano – Freddie Haynes
Drums – Ralph Gleason
Bass – Lawrence Wootten
Guitar – Ray Lanham

StriPe
Nashville, Tennessee

FRED ROSE MUSIC
BMI
1:49

RECORD NO.
501
(srp 4400)

LONG GONE LONESOME BLUES
(Hank Williams)
HOLLIS CHAMPION

Brunswick
(REGD.)
MADE IN ENGLAND FOR BRUNSWICK LTD

CINEPHONIC
MUSIC

R/T
9198
05317

THIRTEEN WOMEN
(Thompson)
BILL HALEY AND HIS
COMETS
Vocal, Bill Haley

TAIL
RECO

SIDE A
T-1005

JACK BAYMOORE
A-V8
(K

ULTRA HIGH FIDELITY

KENT

45x314
Vocal
Jesse James
2:20

ub.
Music
-2)

RED HOT ROCKIN BLUES
(Lee and Jim Denson)
JESSE JAMES

KENT RECORDS • CULVER CITY • CALIF.

JAN
nob
© 1980

JAN 45-030 A

HASIL ADKINS
SHE'S MINE
(H Adkins)
Activ, ASCAP

Capitol
REG. U.S. PAT. OFF.

Central Songs, Inc.
BMI-2:21
F3461

Vocal with
Instrumental
Accompaniment
(45-15464)

HEART-BREAKIN' MAMA
(McDonald-Stewart-Howard)
SKEETS McDONALD

MANUFACTURED BY CAPITOL RECORDS INC. • HOLLYWOOD, CALIFORNIA • U.S.A.

METEOR
RECORDS

(MR 5045) 2:17
Mar Publ
BMI

Vocal
Jr Thompson

MAMA'S LITTLE BABY
(Thompson, O. Clausch)
JUNIOR THOMPSON
with
THE METEORS
5029

ABC-PARAMOUNT

45-9714
AMP 45-1011

Cedarwood Publ.
Co., Inc. BMI
2:10

Vocal with
Instrumental
Accompaniment

PRETTY BAD BLUES
(Self)
RONNIE SELF

A PRODUCT OF AM-PAR RECORD CORP.

KING

K4058
(Anna-BMI)
K-4927